HOLIDAYS & HEROES

Let's Celebrate

COLUMBUS DAY

BY Barbara deRubertis

ILLUSTRATED BY Thomas Sperling

CHRISTOPHER COLUMBUS

The Kane Press • New York

For activities and resources for this book and others in the HOLIDAYS & HEROES series, visit: www.kanepress.com/holidays-and-heroes

Library of Congress Cataloging-in-Publication Data

deRubertis, Barbara.
[Columbus Day]
Let's celebrate Columbus Day / by Barbara deRubertis ; illustrated by Thomas Sperling. -- Revised edition.
    pages cm. -- (Holidays & heroes)
Original edition published: 1992.
Original edition has subtitle: Let's meet Christopher Columbus.
ISBN 978-1-57565-634-2 (pbk. : alk. paper) -- ISBN 978-1-57565-725-7 (library reinforced edition : alk. paper)
1. Columbus Day--Juvenile literature. 2. Columbus, Christopher--Juvenile literature. 3. America--Discovery and exploration--Spanish--Juvenile literature. I. Sperling, Thomas, 1952- illustrator. II. Title.
E120.D47 2013
394.264--dc23
                            2013001682

eISBN: 978-1-57565-635-9

1 3 5 7 9 10 8 6 4 2

Revised edition first published in the United States of America in 2014 by Kane Press, Inc.
Printed in the United States of America

Book Design: Edward Miller
Photograph/Image Research: Maura Taboubi

Christopher Columbus was born around 1450 in Genoa, a city that is now part of the country of Italy.

Christopher's father was a weaver of cloth. He wanted Christopher to be a weaver, too. But Christopher dreamed of being a sailor. Finally, his father agreed.

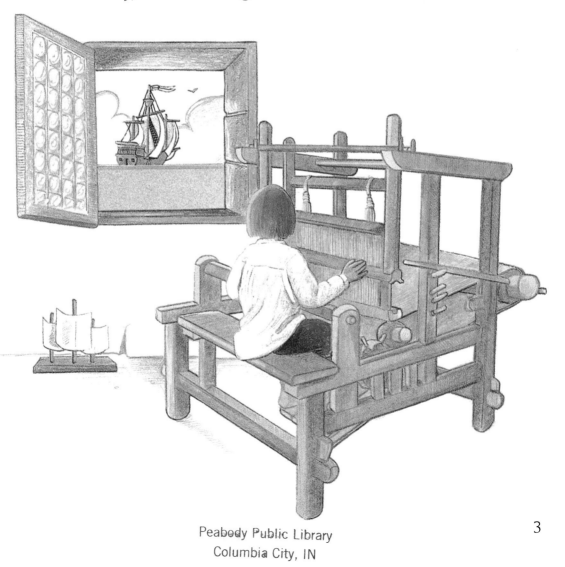

By the time Christopher Columbus was twenty-five years old, he had sailed many places. He worked trading goods with people along the coasts of Europe and West Africa.

As Columbus traveled, he learned several languages. He spoke with other sailors. He read books about geography, astronomy, religion, and history.

But Columbus was especially interested in a book written by Marco Polo.

Marco Polo had traveled east from Italy, over land, to countries then called "the Indies." He described the riches he found in India, China, and Japan. Silks. Spices. And *gold*!

Columbus wanted to find these riches, too. So he began making a plan to travel to the Indies. But he would not go **east** over land like Marco Polo. He would sail **west** over the ocean!

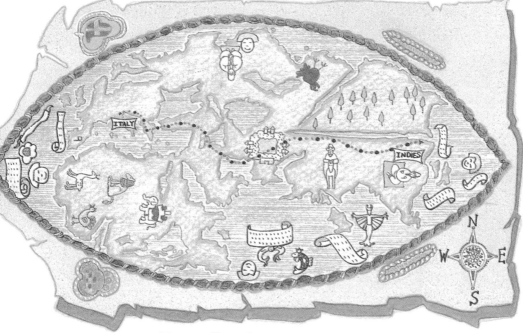

MARCO POLO'S JOURNEY EAST • • •>

It was a daring plan . . . but it had problems!

Most of the maps that were available at that time showed a world that was much smaller than it really is. Columbus figured that he would cross the "Ocean Sea" (now called the Atlantic Ocean) and land in China.

Columbus did not know that after crossing the Ocean Sea, he would bump into two continents that were unknown to him and to most people in Europe. These continents were later named North America and South America.

The Americas were already home to many people. Thousands of years earlier, settlers had traveled across a land bridge to what is now Alaska. They then spread out across the two continents. Over time, the land bridge was covered with water.

Also, about 500 years before Columbus dreamed of sailing west, Viking explorers had done so. They made settlements in Greenland and Canada that lasted hundreds of years.

But people in southern Europe knew little or nothing about the Viking voyages.

Columbus knew his journey would be difficult
and possibly dangerous. Most sailors thought
the Ocean Sea was too wide for a safe voyage
to the Indies. Also, the plan was expensive and
Columbus did not have enough money.

In 1484, he asked the King of Portugal for help.

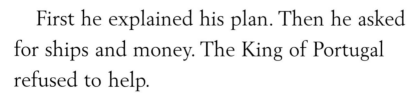

First he explained his plan. Then he asked for ships and money. The King of Portugal refused to help.

Columbus went back to the king and asked for ships and money a second time. Again the King of Portugal said no.

Columbus was disappointed. But he was not willing to give up on his plan. So in 1486, he went to see King Ferdinand and Queen Isabella of Spain. They listened to Columbus. Then they asked a committee to study his plan.

Columbus appears before Queen Isabella and the Court of Spain.

After four long years, the committee finally reached a decision.

They said no.

Columbus was *very* disappointed.

But he was also *very* determined!

He went back to see the King and Queen of Spain.

The king and queen again listened to Columbus. He told them about the colonies he could establish for Spain. About the ways he could spread Christianity. About the riches he could bring home. Silk. Spices. And *gold*!

Columbus tried to convince them. But once again the king and queen said no.

Next, Columbus decided
to visit the King of France.
He was on his way when a
messenger caught up with him. The messenger
told Columbus to come back. The King and
Queen of Spain had changed their minds!

It was now 1492.
After eight long years,
Columbus's dream
was finally in reach!

The king and queen signed an agreement with Columbus. They gave him a title: Grand Admiral of the Ocean Sea. They promised to make him governor of all the lands he might conquer. And they promised to give him a share of all the treasures he brought back to Spain. Columbus was quite pleased.

Columbus speaks with Queen Isabella and King Ferdinand.

    The king and queen also gave Columbus
three ships:
       the *Niña,*
       the *Pinta,*
       and the *Santa Maria.*
    Columbus chose to sail on the *Santa Maria.*
It was the largest.

On August 3, 1492, Columbus sailed from Spain to islands off the coast of Africa. There he gathered more food and supplies, and he made repairs to his ships.

On the 6th of September, he headed west, across the Ocean Sea.

Columbus kept track of days, directions, and distances. His ships sailed farther and farther away from Spain. His sailors grew more and more worried.

A month dragged by with no sight of land.

Columbus navigates by the stars from the deck of the *Santa Maria* in 1492.

The sailors were scared and ready to give up. They wanted to turn around and go home.

But Columbus persuaded them to give him three more days. He was a skilled navigator. He was determined. And he wasn't ready to give up.

They kept on sailing.

Two days later, they saw birds. Columbus changed direction to follow the birds. He hoped they would lead him to land.

Columbus kept watch until late that night.

Finally, at two o'clock in the morning, a
lookout on the *Pinta* saw land and gave a shout.
The captain of the *Pinta* then fired a cannon.
The date was October 12, 1492.

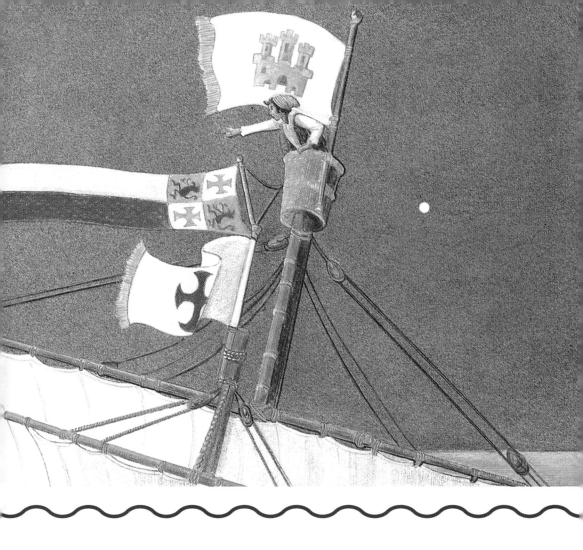

Columbus thought he had found the Indies.
In fact, he had found the Bahamas, islands near
North America and South America.

Columbus and his sailors went ashore. The native people welcomed them. They spoke to each other using sign language. Columbus called the native people "Indians" because he thought he had reached the Indies!

The first native people Columbus met were peaceful and friendly. They gave Columbus and his men delicious food. They also showed them how to make hammocks.

But Columbus was more interested in *gold*.

He saw that many of the native people were wearing gold earrings. He wanted to know where the gold had come from. So he took some of the natives prisoner and forced them to show him. Columbus and his sailors then visited other islands, looking for treasure.

Along the way, Columbus collected things to take home. A small amount of gold. Native birds and plants. And more native prisoners.

He could not bring home the *Santa Maria*. It had wrecked on a coral reef. So he would sail home on the *Niña*.

After six months away, Columbus returned to Spain. Most people had thought he would never come back. When he did return, he was welcomed as a great hero.

Columbus was very happy about his successful voyage.

But he wanted more. Especially more gold!

The King and Queen of Spain sent Columbus on three more voyages west. But each voyage brought more and more trouble.

Columbus and his men treated the native people very badly. And they were treated badly in return.

Also, huge numbers of native people died from diseases carried by Columbus's men and cargo—European diseases like smallpox, measles, and chicken pox. The native people had no resistance to these diseases.

Columbus was tired and sick when he completed his last voyage.

He had never found the large amounts of gold and riches he had promised King Ferdinand and Queen Isabella. And because he had not been a good governor of the colonies, he had been removed from his position of power.

Also, Columbus never realized that he had "bumped into" the two large continents of North America and South America. He still believed he had been exploring the Indies!

A Columbus Day parade in New York City

When Christopher Columbus died in 1506, he was a forgotten man. But today, he is remembered for his famous first voyage to the Americas.

Columbus Day, on October 12, became a federal holiday in 1937. Later, the holiday was moved to the second Monday in October.

In some places, Columbus Day is celebrated with parades. Other places do not recognize the holiday at all. Some people celebrate Native American Day or Indigenous Peoples Day instead.

A Native American Day celebration in South Dakota

Many have written that Columbus sailed from the "Old World" and discovered a "New World." But it is probably more accurate to say he discovered another Old World. He then introduced these two worlds to each other. This created a much larger, more diverse, and more interesting New World!

Later, millions of people would follow his example and travel to the Americas.

Whether or not we celebrate Columbus Day, we can admire the amazing navigation skills of Christopher Columbus. We can admire his determination. And we can admire the huge accomplishment of opening a pathway between continents unknown to each other.

We can learn from what Columbus did right, as well as from what he did wrong.

For thousands of years people have traveled between the continents—over land and across the seas. Along the way, they have shared goods and ideas. And they have learned many things about one another.

On Columbus Day, we can remember to respect and protect all the lands, waters, and people we encounter as we explore our world.